THE STORY OF
DISNEY

ADELE RICHARDSON

A$^+$

Published by Smart Apple Media
1980 Lookout Drive, North Mankato, Minnesota 56003

Photography by Corbis (AFP, Bettmann, Corbis Sygma, Douglas Kirkland, James
Leynse/Corbis SABA, Roman Soumar, Peter Turnley, Forestier Yves), Icon SMI
(John Cordes), Sally McCrae Kuyper, Photofest (Walt Disney Productions), PRNews
Foto (Disney Enterprises, Inc./Pixar Animation Studios), Time Life Pictures/
Getty Images (Alfred Eisenstaedt, J. R. Eyerman, Yale Joel, Erica Lanser/
Black Star, Peter Stackpole), Unicorn Stock Photos (Mark E. Gibson)

Library of Congress Cataloging-in-Publication Data
Richardson, Adele.
The story of Disney / by Adele Richardson.
p. cm. — (Built for success)
Summary: Discusses the history of the Walt Disney Company and
the life and career of Walt Disney.
ISBN 1-58340-291-8
1. Walt Disney Company—History—Juvenile literature. 2. Disney,
Walt, 1901-1966—Juvenile literature. [1. Walt Disney Company—
History. 2. Disney, Walt, 1901-1966. 3. Motion pictures—Biography.] I. Title. II. Series.
PN1999.W27 R53 2003
384.8'0979494—dc21
2002030980

First Edition
2 4 6 8 9 7 5 3 1

THE STORY OF
DISNEY

Table of Contents

Disney Today

In July 1923, Walt Disney left home to join his older brother Roy in Hollywood, California. He brought nothing more than a few cartoon drawings, a used suit, and $40. Roy had saved up about $250, and together they borrowed $500 more to set up a **film studio**. The Disney brothers were going to make cartoons, or **animated films**. They bought a second-hand camera and rented a small workspace. A sign in the window read, "Disney Brothers Studio." Few people knew about the small business, but the Disney brothers had plenty of creativity—and a lot of determination.

Disney Brothers Studio eventually became the Walt Disney Company. It grew from making a few hundred dollars in 1923 to more than $25 billion in 2001. Today, many people think of the popular animated films produced by the company when they hear the Disney name. While the film studio is still the heart of the Walt Disney Company, the company is involved in many other entertainment projects.

Many visitors travel to Disneyland in California or Walt Disney World in Florida. The Walt Disney Company also runs

amusement parks in Japan and France. The Epcot (Experimental Prototype Community of Tomorrow) Center in Florida invites visitors to venture into the future and travel to foreign lands. Just down the road is Disney's Animal Kingdom, where visitors can view more than 1,000 animals from around the world, as well as exhibits about dinosaurs and other extinct creatures. The newest Disney amusement park is scheduled to open in 2005 or 2006 in Hong Kong, China.

The Disney Company receives billions of dollars in **royalties** every year. People and businesses who use pictures of

The Disney theme parks bring fantasy to life

Disney characters, show Disney movies, play Disney music, or otherwise use Disney's property must pay a fee to the Walt Disney Company. Millions of people all over the world know and love Mickey Mouse, Donald Duck, Goofy, and the many other famous Disney characters. The popularity of Disney's characters encourages many companies to feature their pictures on products.

Disney also has its own store that sells products with the company name and characters. In 2001, the Disney Store had about 700 locations in nine countries. That same year, more than 250 million people all over the world visited the stores to purchase Disney **merchandise**.

When Americans watch television, many of them tune in to a Disney production. Disney owns the ABC **television**

Mickey Mouse

Mickey Mouse is an international movie star, but not everyone knows him by the same name. Italians call him *Pololino*, which means "Little Mouse." Spanish fans call him *El Raton Mickey*—the Spanish words for "Mickey the Mouse." Here are a few names for the world's most famous mouse and the languages from which they come.

Miki Maus	Bulgarian	*Miki Tikus*	Indonesian
Mi Lau Shu	Chinese	*Myszka Mickey*	Polish
Mikki Maous	Greek	*Musse Pigg*	Swedish
Miki Egér	Hungarian		

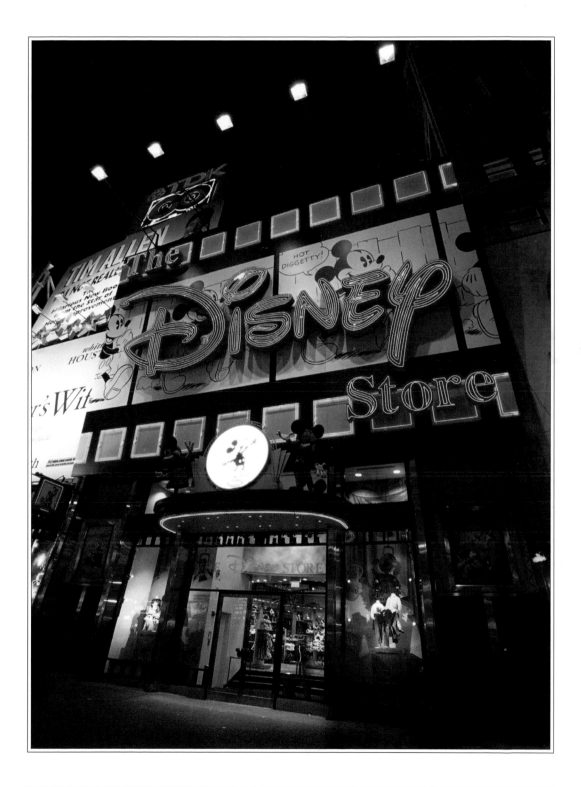

Disney stores sell clothes, toys, movies, and more

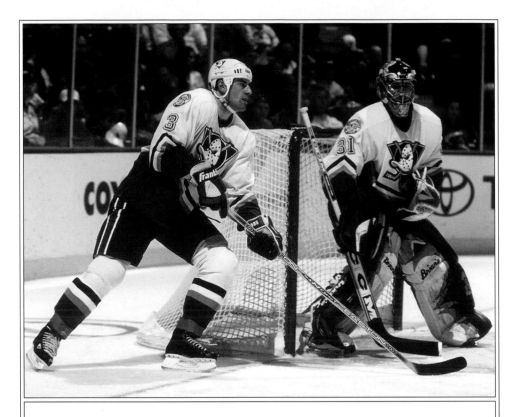

network, with stations across the United States. Disney also owns several cable companies. Besides the Disney Channel, the Walt Disney Company enjoys part ownership in cable networks such as the History Channel, Arts and Entertainment (A&E), Lifetime Television, and E! Entertainment Television. Disney has also started television stations and cable channels in many other parts of the world, including Europe, Asia, South America, and Australia.

For sports fans, there's the Mighty Ducks of Anaheim, a National Hockey League team owned by Disney. The

The Mighty Ducks won 29 games in the 2001–2002 season

Anaheim Angels, a Major League Baseball team, is also partially owned by the company. Many other sports can be seen on ESPN and ESPN2, two more Disney networks. Monday Night Football, an ABC program, belongs to Disney as well.

Many Americans listen to Disney-owned radio programs and stations. In addition to Disney Radio and ESPN Radio, Disney provides programming to more than 4,600 radio stations across the United States. Companies that advertise their products on Disney television, cable, and radio stations pay the Walt Disney Company billions of dollars each year.

The Disney Channel airs movies such as *Beauty and the Beast*

Disney is the world's largest publisher of children's books and magazines. It also publishes books read by adults. In 2001, more than 100 million people in 74 different countries bought books and magazines published by a Disney company. Miramax Books, Hyperion Books, and Walt Disney Company Book Publishing are three names that Disney uses to publish and market books. There are also nearly 20 magazine titles that Disney owns or partially owns. Some popular Disney magazines are *Discover*, *Biography*, and *ESPN Magazine*.

Theatergoers can see stage productions of *Beauty and the Beast* and *The Lion King* all over the world. The cast and crew members of these productions travel from city to city, putting on shows for thousands of people to see each week.

In 1994, the Disney Cruise Line was formed. The Cruise Line has two ships, named the *Disney Magic* and the *Disney Wonder*. Each cruise ship is more than 950 feet (290 m) long and can hold up to 1,750 passengers. Guests can eat in a different Disney-themed restaurant every night and choose from many activities. On the last day of a cruise the ships stop at Castaway Cay, a private island owned by Disney.

Disney cruise stops include Key West in Florida

Guests can rent boats, take hikes, or relax on the beach. The only way to get to Castaway Cay is to take a Disney cruise.

The Walt Disney Company is nearly everywhere in the entertainment world. It is one of many businesses that developed from the vision and work of only a few people. In this case, the person most responsible for Disney's success was Walter Elias Disney. It is impossible to tell the story of the Walt Disney Company without telling his story as well.

Castaway Cay offers snorkeling and parasailing

Mickey Mouse and Walt Disney

A multibillion-dollar company seldom starts at the top, and success doesn't always come quickly. Sometimes a company's **founders** struggle for many years before achieving their goals. Walt Disney had his share of hard times before he finally achieved success.

Walter Elias Disney was born on December 5, 1901, in Chicago, Illinois. He was the fourth son of Elias and Flora Disney. Walt's parents were not happy living in their neighborhood because they didn't think it was safe to raise a family there. When Walt was five years old, two local boys were arrested for killing a policeman. His parents had finally had enough and quickly packed up everything. They moved the family to a farm in Marceline, Missouri.

Walt and his younger sister Ruth especially loved life on the farm. Since they were so young, the two had few chores and could spend much of their time playing on the 45-acre (18.5 ha) farm. Unfortunately, Walt's father became very sick and was unable to keep the farm running. In 1911, the family sold the farm and moved to Kansas City.

Mickey Mouse turned 75 years old in 2003

While in Kansas City, Walt's father bought a newspaper route. Walt and one of his older brothers, Roy, got up at 3:30 every morning to deliver papers. Walt's father did not want them to throw the papers on people's lawns like other boys. They had to walk up to each house and place a paper behind the customer's storm door. This lesson in making every effort to keep customers happy left a deep impression on the boys. It gave them a drive for perfection that would stay with them the rest of their lives.

Walt's artistic career didn't begin smoothly. His first job as a commercial artist, for $50 a month, ended quickly because there wasn't enough business. At age 19, he started his first company with an artist friend named Ub Iwerks. Their company, Iwerks-Disney Commercial Artists, lasted only one month before they accepted offers to work for the Kansas City Slide Company. When they saved enough money to go out on their own again, Walt and Ub started another company, called Laugh-O-Gram Films. Within a year, the company was forced into **bankruptcy** because Walt and Ub didn't make enough money to pay their bills.

In 1923, Walt decided to move to Hollywood and make films with his brother Roy. The two signed a contract with a company in New York to make cartoons. Walt created the animation drawings, and his brother worked the camera. The brothers hired two young women to paint the **celluloid**, and Roy photographed the celluloid onto **film**.

In 1924, Ub moved to California to take over the animation duties. Two years later, the brothers changed the studio's name to Walt Disney Studio. The Disney brothers and Ub struggled to get enough work just to pay themselves and their few employees. Sometimes it looked like they wouldn't make it.

Walt wouldn't quit, though. His dedication to creativity carried him through the early difficulties. After five long years of struggling, the Walt Disney Studio got its big break. Walt was returning by train to California from New York City. During the trip, he was sketching in his drawing book, looking for new ideas, when suddenly he had an inspiration. He created a cartoon character named Mickey Mouse. The new character saved the studio. Walt later said, "Mickey Mouse popped out

Above, Disney animators make thousands of drawings;
left, Walt Disney editing *Pinnochio*; right, sketching at his desk

of my mind and on a drawing pad on a train ride at a time when the business fortunes of my brother Roy and myself were low and disaster seemed right around the corner . . . the little fellow provided the means for expanding our organization."

In the early days of the film industry, movies did not have sound. Mickey Mouse was supposed to make his first appearance in a silent film called *Plane Crazy*. Just before

Making a Cartoon

A cartoon begins with an idea for a story. Then writers create a script of what will happen. Once the writers have worked out a plot for the story, sound engineers plan a musical script. Usually all the sound—including voices, sound effects, and background music—is created before the animation work begins so that animators, the people who draw the cartoons, can match the action to the soundtrack.

The animators sketch their ideas on story boards. They draw the action for each scene. Their first drawings, called conceptual drawings, show what the film and its characters will look like. Animators work on the characters for many hours to create different emotions and movements. Often, three-dimensional models are made out of clay so the animators can see how the character would look from different angles. Then layout artists design the settings, the action, and the camera angles and shots.

Finally, the animators draw backgrounds, characters, and special effects in pencil. When everyone finishes their work, they run the pencil drawings through a test to check if the animation works as planned. If everything looks good, clean-up artists finish the animation. They make color pictures based on the pencil drawings. When the animation is combined with its soundtrack, the film is ready for the movie theaters.

Today's animated films are usually created with the help of computers, but creativity and imagination are still the keys to any successful film.

Plane Crazy came out, filmmakers learned how to make movies with **soundtracks**. Disney set aside *Plane Crazy* and made a short film called *Steamboat Willie* instead.

Steamboat Willie debuted in 1928. It was the world's first cartoon with sound. Walt himself supplied Mickey's squeaky voice. Almost overnight, millions of Mickey Mouse fans were born. "Mickey Mouse Clubs" sprung up across the country. On Saturday afternoons, young people attended club meetings at local theaters. They sang Mickey Mouse songs, traded souvenirs, and watched the latest cartoons.

The first Mickey Mouse doll was sold in 1930

The Walt Disney Studio grew on the success of Mickey Mouse. The studio created many other imaginative cartoon characters, such as Pluto, Donald Duck, and Goofy, and made dozens of movies, including *Snow White and the Seven Dwarfs*, *Pinocchio*, and *Fantasia*. It also produced one of the first color television shows, *The Wonderful World of Color*.

In 1955, Disneyland opened in Anaheim, California. Within 10 years, 30 million people had visited Disneyland. By then, Walt was creating two new parks in Florida: Walt Disney World and Epcot, which he imagined as the city of tomorrow.

Pinocchio's Jiminy Cricket is a popular Disney character

Life After Walt

Walt didn't live to see Walt Disney World or Epcot completed. He died of lung cancer in 1966 at the age of 65. His brother Roy became the **chief executive officer** (CEO) of the Walt Disney Company until his death in 1971. But the company continued to travel along the road Walt and Roy had paved. Disney's president from 1971 through 1980, Carl Walker, completed Walt's work on the new theme parks. Walt Disney World opened in October 1971 and was followed by Epcot Center in October 1982.

The theme parks continued to be very successful, but people were becoming less interested in the types of family films Disney produced. As a result, the company was losing audiences to other film companies that made movies teenagers and adults wanted to see. Disney had to do something to keep up with the competition.

In an effort to get the company moving again, its leaders formed Touchstone Pictures. Instead of making movies that appealed only to children and young families, Touchstone would make movies for young adults and older audiences. In

The "Spaceship Earth" pavilion at Epcot Center is globe-shaped

1984, Touchstone released its first film, *Splash*, starring Tom Hanks and Darryl Hannah. The movie was a huge hit. Touchstone has continued its success with such films as *Pearl Harbor*, starring Ben Affleck, *Signs*, starring Mel Gibson, and *Armageddon*, starring Bruce Willis.

Touchstone was a step in the right direction, but it wasn't enough. In September 1984, the Walt Disney Company hired Michael Eisner as its chairman and CEO. When Disney hired him, Eisner was working for Paramount Pictures—one of the biggest entertainment companies in the world. With Eisner as its leader, Paramount made many popular movies, including *Raiders of the Lost Ark* and three of the *Star Trek* films. Not only were his films successful, but Eisner was able to make them for less than what other companies spent.

Under Eisner's direction, Disney founded or gained through **acquisitions** a number of other film and entertainment companies, including Hollywood Pictures, Miramax Films, and Hollywood Records. In 1995, the Walt Disney Company made an even bigger decision. Disney became the largest entertainment company in the world when it bought Capital Cities/ABC

Television for about $19 billion in a **merger**. After the merger, Disney owned all the ABC television programs and many other entertainment **media**.

Disney has become so large that it is organized into many companies. Each has its own job to do and its own president. One Disney company works only on feature-length movies. Another company manages Disneyland and the other theme parks. Separate Disney companies produce plays for the theater, manage the television stations, and handle the cable networks. Still more companies oversee home videos, DVDs, and

Touchstone Pictures' *Pearl Harbor* was a blockbuster hit

Disney characters appear onscreen, onstage, and in print

video games. Disney's music company produces popular music. Its publishing company creates books that feature popular Disney characters.

Disney was able to get the money to buy other companies in several ways. Part of the money was its own, and part of it was borrowed. Some of the money also came from the thousands of people who own a portion of the Walt Disney Company. Disney is a **publicly traded company**, which means that people throughout the world can buy and sell **stock** in it. Anyone may own part of the Walt Disney Company by purchasing shares of its stock.

Disney has sold stock in the company for a long time. In 1940, after the release of *Snow White and the Seven Dwarfs* and *Pinocchio*, the company wanted to raise money for new projects. Walt and Roy offered 600,000 shares of stock to the public for five dollars each, raising $3 million. People buy stock in a company because they hope the value of the stock will increase. They hope to sell their stock at a higher price than they bought it. The Walt Disney Company has made profits for its stockholders for many years.

Japan's second Disney theme park opened in 2001

Over the years, the Walt Disney Company has kept its stock valuable by finding ways to expand its business. One way the company has grown is by opening new theme parks in different parts of the world. Tokyo Disneyland opened in Japan in 1983, and Disneyland Paris opened in 1992. Each of these parks has already been visited by millions of people, with millions more planning to visit in the future.

Disney has also grown by getting involved with the Internet. In 1995, the Walt Disney Internet Group was formed. This company manages several of the Internet's most popular sites, including Disney.com, ESPN.com, and ABCnews.com. People go to these and many other Disney-managed sites to find news and information and play games. Vacation reservations for Disney's parks, resorts, and cruises can be made on DisneyVacations.com.

Walt Disney Studios has expanded over the years, too. The company took a new turn in moviemaking in 1991 when it began working with a company called Pixar. Disney and Pixar created the world's first fully computer-animated feature film. Computers had been used to help with animation before, but

this time the movie was made from start to finish with computers doing all the animation work. After four years, the film *Toy Story* finally opened in theaters. The film has been so popular that it has made more than $350 million worldwide. Disney and Pixar also created *Toy Story 2* and *A Bug's Life*, and plan to create at least one more computer-animated film together. Disney has also continued to create traditional animated films, such as *Tarzan, Atlantis: The Lost Empire*, and *Lilo & Stitch*.

The Walt Disney Company has come a long way since Walt created Mickey Mouse. On October 1, 2001, Walt Disney

Toy Story stars two toy action figures named Buzz and Woody

Above, *Armageddon*'s all-star cast included Bruce Willis;
below, Disney and Pixar released *Monsters, Inc.* in 2001

World began a 15-month long celebration to honor Walt's imagination and creativity, 100 years after his birth. The celebration was called "100 Years of Magic" and featured special parades and shows at all four parks in Orlando, Florida. At the Disney-MGM (Metro Goldwyn Mayer) Studios, a new attraction opened to pay tribute to the company's founder. Items from the Disney **archives** that had never been seen by the public were put on display. Visitors could also experience a new show, called "Walt Disney: One Man's Dream." The show told the story of Walt Disney, his company, and how the Disney company has grown over the years, as well as some of its plans for the future.

From Idea to Screen

The word "animation" means "creating life." Artists draw many thousands of individual pictures. Next they transfer the pictures one at a time to film. When they run the film through a projector at high speed, the drawings appear to move. The pictures aren't really moving, of course. The human eye fills in the gaps so that, for example, a lion appears to be running through the jungle.

Young artists can create their own animation by drawing a stick-figure lion in the corner of a pad of paper. On each page of the pad, the lion's legs should be drawn in a position slightly different from the position on the pages before. When the pages of the pad are fanned quickly, the lion appears to be walking!

Disney in the World

The Walt Disney Company has its critics as well as its supporters when it comes to **corporate citizenship**. Disney, like most large companies in the United States, wants its customers to see the company as a good citizen that helps members of its community. Some people who run large companies genuinely believe corporations, like people, should have a conscience. A good corporate citizen treats its employees fairly and protects the environment. It gives money back to the community and encourages its employees to do volunteer work.

The Walt Disney Company has a policy of good citizenship. Disney treats its employees well and has strong **minority hiring practices**. African-Americans and women hold important positions at Disney companies, and Disney hires many minority writers and directors to work on its film and television projects.

Since 1983, Disney has sponsored a program called VoluntEARS (named for Mickey Mouse's famous ears). Every week of the year, Disneyland employees voluntarily provide meals to the elderly in southern California communities. They

Walt Disney World's grand opening was held in 1971

help raise money for cancer research, actively take part in community programs, and work with children and young people who are at risk.

During 2001, in places across the world, more than 85,000 Disney employees contributed 350,000 volunteer hours. Some VoluntEARS work with the Boys & Girls Club of America to remodel clubhouses, take kids on field trips, and help kids with homework and after-school activities. Volunteers from Disneyland have worked on projects to turn vacant city lots into playgrounds and raised money for local children's hospitals. Three times a week, volunteers from Walt Disney World in Florida cook and serve meals to people who are homeless.

Support for Disney's volunteer work is universal, but some people believe the Walt Disney Company does not always make the right choices. Many organizations are unhappy with Disney because of violence featured on its children's television shows. They believe Disney and other producers of children's entertainment should eliminate violence from all their television and movie projects.

Some critics say that Disney's films are not always accurate. Historians complained that *Pocahontas*, for example, was not true to the real-life story of its heroine. Not everyone wants a Disney park near his or her home, either. Citizens of Virginia protested when the company planned to build a historical theme park called Disney's America in a rural area 30 miles (48 km) from Washington, D.C. The company estimated that an additional 77,000 cars per day would travel through the area. People worried that Disney's plans would increase traffic, pollution, and noise near their homes. Others worried that Disney would not take care to make the park historically accurate. The Walt Disney Company eventually canceled its plans.

Other people have accused Disney of **exploiting** workers in other countries. Disney hires companies in Asia to make

Fantasia

Disney produced and released its first full-length cartoon movie, *Fantasia*, between 1938 and 1940. The project began as a short feature called *The Sorcerer's Apprentice*. Then a famous composer named Leopold Stokowski convinced Walt Disney to let him select famous classical music to use with cartoons. It became a full-length animated feature. But moviegoers thought *Fantasia* was too long. It cost more than $2 million, and Disney lost money when it was first released. Today, however, *Fantasia* is considered a classic. Film critics and young movie fans alike praise the animated film for its creativity.

Many of Disney's products are made overseas

Disney clothing, which it then sells at a profit throughout the world. Many Asian factories pay such low wages that their employees live in poverty—even when they work long hours. Critics believe Disney should either stop making clothes in Asia, or, better yet, insist that the factories it uses pay employees a fair wage.

Everyone agrees that the Walt Disney Company has grown dramatically since Mickey Mouse first appeared in movie theaters to delighted audiences back in 1928. Walt Disney wanted his original love for animation and entertain-

Walt Disney and his wife owed a lot to Mickey Mouse

ment to live on as the company expanded. Toward the end of his life, Walt said, "I only hope that we don't lose sight of one thing—it was all started by a mouse!"

The Walt Disney Company is making every effort to keep alive the imagination and vision of Walt, his brother Roy, and the others who worked so hard to build the company. With animated successes such as *The Lion King, Toy Story*, and many other highly praised films, not to mention its successful theme parks and other forms of entertainment, the Walt Disney Company has good reason to believe that Walt and the other founders would be proud of its continued success.

The Lion King continued Disney's tradition of animated films

1893   Roy Disney, Walt Disney's brother, is born on June 24.

1901   Walter Elias Disney is born on December 5.

1923   Walt Disney leaves for Hollywood. He and his brother Roy sign a contract to make animated films.

1926   Roy and Walt rename their company Walt Disney Studio.

1928   Mickey Mouse makes his debut in *Steamboat Willie*, the world's first synchronized sound cartoon. Fans begin to join Mickey Mouse Clubs around the United States.

1931   Membership in the Mickey Mouse Clubs reaches one million.

1937   Disney releases *Snow White and the Seven Dwarfs*.

1940   Walt and Roy decide to sell stock in the Walt Disney Company.

1955   Disneyland opens in July. *The Mickey Mouse Club* debuts on television in October.

1966   Walt Disney dies on December 15. Walt's brother Roy takes over the company.

1971   Walt Disney World opens in Florida. Roy Disney dies on December 20.

1982   Epcot Center opens in Florida.

1983   Tokyo Disneyland opens.

1984   Michael Eisner takes over as Disney's CEO. Touchstone Pictures' first movie, *Splash*, opens in theaters.

1992   Disneyland Paris opens.

1995   The Walt Disney Company acquires Capitol Cities/ABC Television and becomes the largest entertainment company in the world.

1998   Disney's Animal Kingdom opens in Florida.

2001   The Walt Disney Company begins a 15-month long celebration of Walt's 100th birthday.

Mickey Mouse is everywhere at Disneyland Paris

acquisitions When one company, usually a bigger company, buys (acquires) other companies.

animated films Drawings produced on film and then shown through a projector so that they seem to come alive. Animated films are also called cartoons.

archives Collections of letters, papers, pictures, and recordings kept for historical interest.

bankruptcy When a company (or individual) cannot pay its debts, it may be forced to go out of business. It then pays its debts by selling its property. This process is called bankruptcy.

celluloid Clear, plastic sheets used to make cartoons before computers were developed. Cartoons were painted on celluloid and then photographed onto film, which ran through a projector to display the images on a movie screen.

chief executive officer The person responsible for managing a company and for making decisions that will help the company to make a profit.

corporate citizenship The belief that a corporation should be an honest and contributing member of society. A good corporate citizen treats its employees well, protects the environment, donates some of its earnings back to the community, and helps out in the places where it does business.

exploiting Taking advantage of someone or something for one's own gain.

film A roll of thin, flexible, transparent material coated with a chemical substance. Film is used to take pictures, as with a camera.

film studio A company that makes movies.

founders The people who set up or start a business or organization.

media All the different ways of communicating information to the public, including newspapers, television, radio, books, magazines, and movies.

merchandise Products that are bought or sold.

merger An agreement in which two companies join forces and become one company.

minority hiring practices Guidelines used by a company to make sure that minorities, such as African-Americans or American Indians, have the same opportunities as other groups of people.

publicly traded company A company that sells shares of stock to the public in order to earn money for its business.

royalties Money paid to a company (or person) in exchange for the use of its property.

soundtracks Thin strips on a film that carry sound recording synchronized with, or matched to, the pictures and actions.

stock Shared ownership in a company by many people who buy shares, or portions, of stock, hoping that the company will make a profit and the stock value will increase.

television network A television or cable company that produces programs to be shown on local stations across a large territory. The ABC network, for example, broadcasts its programs on stations all over the United States.

INDEX

Books

Greene, Katherine, and Richard Greene. *Inside the Dream: The Personal Story of Walt Disney*. New York: Disney Editions, 2001.

Isbouts, Jean-Pierre. *Discovering Walt: The Magical Life of Walt Disney*. New York: Disney Editions, 2001.

Lockman, Darcy. *Computer Animation*. New York: Benchmark Books, 2001.

Nardo, Don. *Walt Disney*. San Diego, Calif.: Kidhaven, 2003.

Web Sites

The official Web site of the Walt Disney Company
http://www.disney.com

The Walt Disney Family Museum
http://disney.go.com/disneyatoz/waltdisney/home.html

The Magic of Walt Disney Imagineering
http://www.wdimagic.com